To Matthew Wallace K.W.

*To everyone who loves bears
and works to protect them* B.F.

*The publishers would like
to thank Dr. Christopher Servheen
of the University of Montana for
his help and advice.*

First U.S. edition 1994
Published in Great Britain in 1994 by
Walker Books Ltd., London.

Library of Congress Cataloging-in-Publication Data

Wallace, Karen.
Bears in the forest / by Karen Wallace ; illustrated by
Barbara Firth.—1st U.S. ed.
p.   cm.—(Read and Wonder)
ISBN 1-56402-336-2
1. Bears—Juvenile literature.   2. Bears—Infancy—Juvenile
literature.   3. Parental behavior in animals—Juvenile
literature. [1. Bears.   2. Animals—Infancy.   3. Parental
behavior in animals.]   I. Firth, Barbara, ill.   II. Title.
III. Series.
QL737.C27W36   1994
599.74'446—dc20   93-39668

10 9 8 7 6 5 4 3 2 1

Printed in Italy

The pictures in this book were done in
pencil and watercolor.

Candlewick Press
2067 Massachusetts Avenue
Cambridge, Massachusetts 02140

The bears in this book are black bears. This is the name of their species, but black bears are not always black. They can be reddish, silver, yellow, light brown, or dark brown. Black bears are shy and good-natured animals, and they live in the forests of North America.

BEARS IN THE FOREST

written by
Karen Wallace

CANDLEWICK PRESS
CAMBRIDGE, MASSACHUSETTS

illustrated by
Barbara Firth

Deep in a cave,
a mother bear sleeps.
She is huge and warm.
Her heart beats slowly.
Outside it is cold
and the trees are
covered with snow.
Her newborn cubs
are blind and tiny.
They find her milk
and begin to grow.

Bears sleep through the winter months. This is called hibernation.

A mother bear's cubs are usually born during her winter sleep.

Snow slips from
the trees and melts
on the ground.
The ice has broken
on the lake. Mother
bear wakes. Her long
sleep is over. She leads
her cubs down to
the lakeshore.
She slurps and slurps
the freezing water.

Adult bears are very thirsty when they first leave their dens.

Young cubs are still drinking their mother's milk.

Leaves burst from their
buds. There are frogs'
eggs in the lake. Mother
bear snuffs the air for
strange smells, listens
for strange sounds.
Her cubs know
nothing of the forest.
This is their first spring.
Mother bear must
take care.

A mother bear brings up her cubs all by herself.

Bears are good mothers and protect their cubs fiercely.

The summer sun is hot.
Mother bear sits in
a tree stump. Angry bees
buzz around her head,
and stolen honey drips
from her paws.

Bears love honey so much that they'll

rob a bees' nest even if the stings make them bawl with pain.

Her two skinny bear cubs
wrestle in the long grass.
They whinny and squeal
and roll over and over
away from their mother.
Mother bear growls.

Young bears grow quickly, so

they are often rather thin during the early part of their first summer.

Come back! There are
dangers in the forest!
Her cubs do not hear her.
Mother bear snorts.
She is angry.
She strides across
the meadow and
whacks them with
a heavy paw.

Bears growl, whine, whinny, sniff, snuff, snort, and bawl.

Bears are excellent climbers.

Two frightened bear cubs scramble
up the nearest tree. Mother bear waits
below, still as a statue, listening
to the forest. When she feels safe,
she will call her cubs down.
Mother bear must take care.

They can jump from high branches, too, and land unhurt.

Soon the days grow shorter
and squirrels start to hide acorns.
Bushes are bright with berries.
Seed pods flutter to the ground.
Winter is coming. Mother bear
and her cubs eat everything
they can find.

Bears eat grass shoots, mice, insects, fish, berries, nuts, seeds, and honey.

In the autumn they eat as much as they can to prepare for their winter sleep.

Icy winds blast the forest.
Mother bear plods through the snow.
Her cubs are fat. Their fur is thick.
She chooses a shelter that is dark and
dry, where they will sleep through
the long winter months.

During hibernation,

a bear's temperature drops and her heartbeat slows down.

When spring has
woken the bears again,
mother bear leads her cubs to the river.
She follows a trail worn deep in the ground.
Hundreds of bears have walked this way before her.

Bears use old bear trails whenever they can.

They leave their claw marks on trees as messages to other bears.

The river runs deep and fast.
Mother bear wades in.
Soon a silver trout
flashes in her jaws.
The cubs are hungry.
They wade into
the river and catch
their own fish.

Bears are strong swimmers and good at fishing.

Sometime during their second summer,

Mother bear gobbles berries.
Her cubs are playing where
she can't see them.
They are almost grown.
Soon they will leave her.

Mother bear has taught them
everything she knows.

bear cubs leave their mother to find territories of their own.